let's cook vegetarian

Jenny Stacey

p

Contents

Tomato, Olive & Mozzarella Bruschetta

These simple toasts are filled with colour and flavour. They are great as a speedy starter or delicious as an appetiser with a good red wine.

Serves 4

INGREDIENTS

4 muffins
4 garlic cloves, crushed
2 tbsp butter
1 tbsp chopped basil
4 large, ripe tomatoes
1 tbsp tomato purée (paste)
8 pitted black olives, halved
50 g/$1^3/4$ oz Mozzarella cheese, sliced
salt and pepper
fresh basil leaves, to garnish

DRESSING:
1 tbsp olive oil
2 tsp lemon juice
1 tsp clear honey

1 Cut the muffins in half to give eight thick pieces. Toast the muffin halves under a hot grill (broiler) for 2–3 minutes until golden.

2 Mix the garlic, butter and basil together and spread on to each muffin half.

3 Cut a cross shape at the base of each tomato. Plunge the tomatoes in a bowl of boiling water – this will make the skin easier to peel. After a few minutes, pick each tomato up with a fork and peel away the skin. Chop the tomato flesh and mix with the tomato purée (paste) and olives. Divide the mixture between the muffins.

4 Mix the dressing ingredients and drizzle over each muffin. Arrange the Mozzarella cheese on top and season.

5 Return the muffins to the grill (broiler) for 1–2 minutes until the cheese melts.

6 Garnish with fresh basil leaves and serve at once.

VARIATION

Use balsamic vinegar instead of the lemon juice for an authentic Mediterranean flavour.

2

3

4

Hummus & Garlic Toasts

Hummus is a real favourite spread on these garlic toasts for a delicious starter or as part of a light lunch.

Serves 4

INGREDIENTS

HUMMUS:
400 g/14 oz can chick-peas (garbanzo beans)
juice of 1 large lemon
6 tbsp tahini (sesame seed paste)
2 tbsp olive oil
2 garlic cloves, crushed
salt and pepper
chopped fresh coriander (cilantro) and black olives, to garnish

TOASTS:
1 ciabatta loaf, sliced
2 garlic cloves, crushed
1 tbsp chopped fresh coriander (cilantro)
4 tbsp olive oil

1 To make the hummus, firstly drain the chick-peas (garbanzo beans), reserving a little of the liquid. Put the chick-peas (garbanzo beans) and liquid in a food processor and blend, gradually adding the reserved liquid and lemon juice. Blend well after each addition until smooth.

2 Stir in the tahini (sesame seed paste) and all but 1 teaspoon of the olive oil. Add the garlic, season to taste and blend again until smooth.

3 Spoon the hummus into a serving dish. Drizzle the remaining olive oil over the top, garnish with chopped coriander (cilantro) and olives. Leave to chill in the refrigerator whilst preparing the toasts.

4 Lay the slices of ciabatta on a grill (broiler) rack in a single layer.

5 Mix the garlic, coriander (cilantro) and olive oil together and drizzle over the bread slices. Cook under a hot grill (broiler) for 2–3 minutes until golden brown, turning once. Serve hot with the hummus.

COOK'S TIP

Make the hummus 1 day in advance, and chill, covered, in the refrigerator until required. Garnish and serve.

2

Mixed Bean Pâté

This is a really quick starter to prepare if canned beans are used. Choose a wide variety of beans for colour and flavour or use a can of mixed beans.

Serves 4

INGREDIENTS

- 400 g/14 oz can mixed beans, drained
- 2 tbsp olive oil
- juice of 1 lemon
- 2 garlic cloves, crushed
- 1 tbsp chopped fresh coriander (cilantro)
- 2 spring onions (scallions), chopped
- salt and pepper
- shredded spring onions (scallions), to garnish

1 Rinse the beans thoroughly under cold running water and drain well.

2 Transfer the beans to a food processor or blender and process until smooth. Alternatively, place the beans in a bowl and mash with a fork or potato masher.

3 Add the olive oil, lemon juice, garlic, coriander (cilantro) and spring onions (scallions) and blend until fairly smooth. Season with salt and pepper to taste.

4 Transfer the pâté to a serving bowl and chill for at least 30 minutes. Garnish with shredded spring onions (scallions) and serve.

COOK'S TIP

Use canned beans which have no salt or sugar added and always rinse thoroughly before use.

COOK'S TIP

Serve the pâté with warm pitta bread or granary toast.

2

3

3

Vegetable Enchiladas

This Mexican dish uses prepared tortillas which are readily available in supermarkets. They are filled with a spicy vegetable mixture and topped with a hot tomato sauce.

Serves 4

INGREDIENTS

4 flour tortillas
75 g/2$^{3}/_{4}$ oz/$^{3}/_{4}$ cup vegetarian Cheddar, grated

FILLING:
75 g/2$^{3}/_{4}$ oz spinach
2 tbsp olive oil
8 baby sweetcorn cobs, sliced
25 g/1 oz/1 tbsp frozen peas, thawed
1 red (bell) pepper, diced
1 carrot, diced
1 leek, sliced
2 garlic cloves, crushed
1 red chilli, chopped
salt and pepper

SAUCE:
300 ml/$^{1}/_{2}$ pint/1$^{1}/_{4}$ cups passata (sieved tomatoes)
2 shallots, chopped
1 garlic clove, crushed
300 ml/$^{1}/_{2}$ pint/1$^{1}/_{4}$ cups vegetable stock
1 tsp caster (superfine) sugar
1 tsp chilli powder

1 To make the filling, blanch the spinach in a pan of boiling water for 2 minutes, drain well and chop.

2 Heat the oil in a frying pan (skillet) and sauté the corn, peas, (bell) pepper, carrot, leek, garlic and chilli for 3–4 minutes, stirring briskly. Stir in the spinach and season well with salt and pepper to taste.

3 Put all of the sauce ingredients in a saucepan and bring to the boil, stirring. Cook over a high heat for 20 minutes, stirring, until thickened and reduced by a third.

4 Spoon a quarter of the filling along the centre of each tortilla. Roll the tortillas around the filling and place in an ovenproof dish, seam-side down.

5 Pour the sauce over the tortillas and sprinkle the cheese on top. Cook in a preheated oven, 180°C/350°F/Gas Mark 4, for 20 minutes or until the cheese has melted and browned. Serve immediately.

2

4

4

Vegetable Jambalaya

This dish traditionally contains spicy sausage but it is equally delicious filled with vegetables in this spicy vegetarian version.

Serves 4

INGREDIENTS

- 75 g/2$^3/_4$ oz/$^1/_2$ cup brown rice
- 2 tbsp olive oil
- 2 garlic cloves, crushed
- 1 red onion, cut into eight
- 1 aubergine (eggplant), diced
- 1 green (bell) pepper, diced
- 50 g/1$^3/_4$ oz baby corn cobs, halved lengthwise
- 50 g/1$^3/_4$ oz/$^1/_2$ cup frozen peas
- 100 g/3$^1/_2$ oz small broccoli florets
- 150 ml/5 floz/$^2/_3$ cup vegetable stock
- 225 ml/8 fl oz can chopped tomatoes
- 1 tbsp tomato purée (paste)
- 1 tsp creole seasoning
- $^1/_2$ tsp chilli flakes
- salt and pepper

1 Cook the rice in a saucepan of boiling water for 20 minutes or until cooked through. Drain and set aside.

2 Heat the oil in a heavy-based frying pan (skillet) and cook the garlic and onion for 2–3 minutes, stirring.

3 Add the aubergine (eggplant), (bell) pepper, corn, peas and broccoli to the pan and cook, stirring occasionally, for 2–3 minutes.

4 Stir in the vegetable stock and canned tomatoes, tomato purée (paste), creole seasoning and chilli flakes.

5 Season to taste and cook over a low heat for 15–20 minutes or until the vegetables are tender.

6 Stir the brown rice into the vegetable mixture and cook, mixing well, for 3–4 minutes or until hot. Transfer the vegetable jambalaya to warm serving dishes and serve immediately.

COOK'S TIP

Use a mixture of rice, such as wild or red rice, for colour and texture. Cook the rice in advance for a speedier recipe.

Stuffed Mushrooms

Use large open-cap mushrooms for this recipe for their flavour and suitability for filling.

Serves 4

INGREDIENTS

8 open-cap mushrooms
1 tbsp olive oil
1 small leek, chopped
1 celery stick, chopped
100 g/3½ oz firm tofu (bean curd), diced
1 courgette (zucchini), chopped
1 carrot, chopped
100 g/3½ oz/1 cup wholemeal (whole wheat) breadcrumbs
2 tbsp chopped basil
1 tbsp tomato purée (paste)
2 tbsp pine kernels (nuts)
75 g/2¾ oz/¾ cup vegetarian Cheddar cheese, grated
150 ml/¼ pint/⅔ cup vegetable stock
salt and pepper
green salad, to serve

1 Remove the stalks from the mushrooms and chop finely.

2 Heat the oil in a frying pan (skillet). Add the chopped mushroom stalks, leek, celery, tofu (bean curd), courgette (zucchini) and carrot and cook for 3–4 minutes, stirring.

3 Stir in the breadcrumbs, basil, tomato purée (paste) and pine kernels (nuts). Season with salt and pepper to taste.

4 Spoon the mixture into the mushrooms and top with the cheese.

5 Place the mushrooms in a shallow ovenproof dish and pour the vegetable stock around them.

6 Cook in a preheated oven at 220°C/425°F/Gas Mark 7 for 20 minutes or until cooked through and the cheese has melted. Remove the mushrooms from the dish and serve immediately with a green salad.

COOK'S TIP

Vary the vegetables used for flavour and colour or according to those you have available.

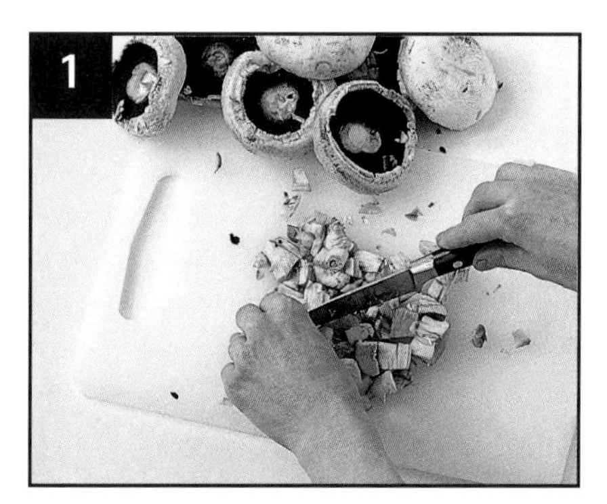

Vegetable Burgers & Chips

These spicy vegetable burgers are delicious, especially when served with the light oven chips (fries). Serve them in a warm bun or roll with radicchio lettuce leaves and red onion relish.

Serves 4

INGREDIENTS

VEGETABLE BURGERS:
100 g/3 1/2 oz spinach
1 tbsp olive oil
1 leek, chopped
2 garlic cloves, crushed
100 g/3 1/2 oz mushrooms, chopped
300 g/10 1/2 oz firm tofu (bean curd), chopped
1 tsp chilli powder
1 tsp curry powder
1 tbsp chopped coriander (cilantro)
75 g/2 3/4 oz fresh wholemeal (whole wheat) breadcrumbs
1 tbsp olive oil

CHIPS (FRIES):
2 large potatoes
2 tbsp flour
1 tsp chilli powder
2 tbsp olive oil
burger bap or roll and salad, to serve

1 To make the burgers, cook the spinach in a little water for 2 minutes. Drain thoroughly and pat dry with paper towels.

2 Heat the oil in a frying pan (skillet) and sauté the leek and garlic for 2–3 minutes. Add the remaining ingredients except for the breadcrumbs and cook for 5–7 minutes until the vegetables have softened. Toss in the spinach and cook for 1 minute.

3 Transfer the mixture to a food processor and blend for 30 seconds until almost smooth. Stir in the breadcrumbs, mixing well, and leave until cool enough to handle. Using floured hands, form the mixture into four equal-sized burgers. Leave to chill for 30 minutes.

4 To make the chips (fries), cut the potatoes into thin wedges and cook in a pan of boiling water for 10 minutes. Drain and toss in the flour and chilli. Lay the chips on a baking tray (cookie sheet) and sprinkle with the oil. Cook in a preheated oven, 200°C/400°F/ Gas Mark 6, for 30 minutes or until golden.

5 Meanwhile, heat 1 tbsp oil in a frying pan (skillet) and cook the burgers for 8–10 minutes, turning once. Serve with salad in a bap.

3

3

4

Lentil Croquettes

These croquettes are ideal served with a crisp salad and a tahini (sesame seed paste) dip.

Serves 4

INGREDIENTS

225 g/8 oz/1 1/4 cups split red lentils
1 green (bell) pepper, finely chopped
1 red onion, finely chopped
2 garlic cloves, crushed
1 tsp garam masala
1/2 tsp chilli powder
1 tsp ground cumin
2 tsp lemon juice
2 tbsp chopped unsalted peanuts
600 ml/1 pint/2 1/2 cups water
1 egg, beaten
3 tbsp plain (all-purpose) flour
1 tsp turmeric
1 tsp chilli powder
4 tbsp vegetable oil
salt and pepper
salad leaves and fresh herbs, to serve

1 Put the lentils in a large saucepan with the (bell) pepper, onion, garlic, garam masala, chilli powder, ground cumin, lemon juice and peanuts.

2 Add the water and bring to the boil. Reduce the heat and simmer for 30 minutes or until the liquid has been absorbed, stirring occasionally.

3 Remove the mixture from the heat and leave to cool slightly. Beat in the egg and season with salt and pepper to taste. Leave to cool completely.

4 With floured hands, form the mixture into eight oblong shapes.

5 Mix the flour, turmeric and chilli powder together on a small plate. Roll the croquettes in the spiced flour mixture to coat.

6 Heat the oil in a large frying pan (skillet) and cook the croquettes, in batches, for 10 minutes, turning once, until crisp on both sides. Serve the croquettes with salad leaves and fresh herbs.

COOK'S TIP

Other lentils could be used, but they will require soaking and precooking before use. Red lentils are used for speed and convenience.

Brown Rice, Vegetable & Herb Gratin

This is a really filling dish and therefore does not require an accompaniment. It is very versatile, and could be made with a wide selection of vegetables.

Serves 4

INGREDIENTS

- 100 g/3½ oz/⅓ cup brown rice
- 2 tbsp butter or margarine
- 1 red onion, chopped
- 2 garlic cloves, crushed
- 1 carrot, cut into matchsticks
- 1 courgette (zucchini), sliced
- 75 g/2¾ oz baby corn cobs, halved lengthwise
- 2 tbsp sunflower seeds
- 3 tbsp chopped mixed herbs
- 100 g/3½ oz/1 cup grated Mozzarella cheese
- 2 tbsp wholemeal (whole wheat) breadcrumbs
- salt and pepper

1 Cook the rice in a saucepan of boiling salted water for 20 minutes. Drain well.

2 Lightly grease a 900 ml/ 1½ pint ovenproof dish.

3 Heat the butter in a frying pan (skillet). Add the onion and cook, stirring, for 2 minutes or until softened.

4 Add the garlic, carrot, courgette (zucchini) and corn cobs and cook for a further 5 minutes, stirring.

5 Mix the rice with the sunflower seeds and mixed herbs and stir into the pan.

6 Stir in half of the Mozzarella cheese and season with salt and pepper to taste.

7 Spoon the mixture into the greased dish and top with the breadcrumbs and remaining cheese. Cook in a preheated oven, 180°C/350°F/Gas Mark 4, for 25–30 minutes or until the cheese begins to turn golden. Serve.

VARIATION

Use an alternative rice, such as basmati, and flavour the dish with curry spices, if you prefer.

4

5

7

Falafel

These are a very tasty, well-known Middle Eastern dish of small chick-pea (garbanzo bean) based balls, spiced and deep-fried. They are delicious hot with a crisp tomato salad.

Serves 4

INGREDIENTS

- 650 g/1 lb 7 oz/6 cups canned chick-peas (garbanzo beans), drained
- 1 red onion, chopped
- 3 garlic cloves, crushed
- 100 g/3 1/2 oz wholemeal (whole wheat) bread
- 2 small red chillies
- 1 tsp ground cumin
- 1 tsp ground coriander
- 1/2 tsp turmeric
- 1 tbsp chopped coriander (cilantro), plus extra to garnish
- 1 egg, beaten
- 100 g/3 1/2 oz/1 cup wholemeal (whole wheat) breadcrumbs
- vegetable oil, for deep-frying
- salt and pepper
- tomato and cucumber salad and lemon wedges, to serve

1 Put the chick-peas (garbanzo beans), onion, garlic, bread, chillies, spices and coriander (cilantro) in a food processor and blend for 30 seconds. Stir and season well.

2 Remove the mixture from the food processor and shape into walnut-sized balls.

3 Place the beaten egg in a shallow bowl and place the wholemeal (wholewheat) breadcrumbs on a plate. Dip the balls into the egg to coat and then roll them in the breadcrumbs, shaking off any excess.

4 Heat the oil for deep-frying to 180°C/350°F or until a cube of bread browns in 30 seconds. Fry the falafel, in batches, for 2–3 minutes until crisp and browned. Remove from the oil with a slotted spoon and dry on absorbent paper towels. Garnish with coriander (cilantro) and serve with a tomato and cucumber salad and lemon wedges.

COOK'S TIP

Serve the falafel with a coriander (cilantro) and yogurt sauce. Mix 150 ml/1/4 pint/2/3 cup natural (unsweetened) yogurt with 2 tbsp chopped coriander (cilantro) and 1 crushed garlic clove.

Kidney Bean Kiev

This is a vegetarian version of chicken kiev, the bean patties taking the place of the chicken. Topped with garlic and herb butter and coated in breadcrumbs, this version is just as delicious.

Serves 4

INGREDIENTS

GARLIC BUTTER:
- 100 g/3½ oz/ 8 tbsp butter
- 3 garlic cloves, crushed
- 1 tbsp chopped parsley

BEAN PATTIES:
- 650 g/1 lb 7 oz canned red kidney beans
- 150 g/5½ oz/1¼ cups fresh white breadcrumbs
- 25 g/1 oz/2 tbsp butter
- 1 leek, chopped
- 1 celery stick, chopped
- 1 tbsp chopped parsley
- 1 egg, beaten
- salt and pepper
- vegetable oil, for shallow frying

1 To make the garlic butter, put the butter, garlic and parsley in a bowl and blend together with a wooden spoon. Place the garlic butter mixture on to a sheet of baking parchment, roll into a cigar shape and wrap in the baking parchment. Leave to chill in the refrigerator.

2 Using a potato masher, mash the red kidney beans in a mixing bowl and stir in 75 g/ 2¾ oz/¾ cup of the breadcrumbs until thoroughly blended.

3 Melt the butter in a frying pan (skillet) and sauté the leek and celery for 3–4 minutes, stirring.

4 Add the bean mixture to the pan together with the parsley, season with salt and pepper to taste and mix well. Remove from the heat and leave to cool slightly.

5 Shape the bean mixture into 4 equal sized ovals.

6 Slice the garlic butter into 4 and place a slice in the centre of each bean patty. Mould the bean mixture around the garlic butter to encase it completely.

7 Dip each bean patty into the beaten egg to coat and then roll in the remaining breadcrumbs.

8 Heat a little oil in a frying pan (skillet) and fry the patties, turning once, for 7–10 minutes or until golden. Serve.

1

6

7

Cashew Nut Paella

Paella traditionally contains chicken and fish, but this recipe is packed with vegetables and nuts for a truly delicious and simple vegetarian dish.

Serves 4

INGREDIENTS

- 2 tbsp olive oil
- 1 tbsp butter
- 1 red onion, chopped
- 150 g/5½ oz/1 cup arborio rice
- 1 tsp ground turmeric
- 1 tsp ground cumin
- ½ tsp chilli powder
- 3 garlic cloves, crushed
- 1 green chilli, sliced
- 1 green (bell) pepper, diced
- 1 red (bell) pepper, diced
- 75 g/2¾ oz baby corn cobs, halved lengthwise
- 2 tbsp pitted black olives
- 1 large tomato, seeded and diced
- 450 ml/¾ pint/2 cups vegetable stock
- 75 g/2¾ oz/¾ cup unsalted cashew nuts
- 25 g/1 oz/¼ cup frozen peas
- 2 tbsp chopped parsley
- pinch of cayenne pepper
- salt and pepper
- fresh herbs, to garnish

1 Heat the olive oil and butter in a large frying pan (skillet) or paella pan until the butter has melted.

2 Add the chopped onion to the pan and sauté for 2–3 minutes, stirring, until the onion has softened.

3 Stir in the rice, turmeric, cumin, chilli powder, garlic, chilli, (bell) peppers, corn cobs, olives and tomato and cook over a medium heat for 1–2 minutes, stirring occasionally.

4 Pour in the stock and bring the mixture to the boil. Reduce the heat and cook for 20 minutes, stirring.

5 Add the cashew nuts and peas to the mixture in the pan and cook for a further 5 minutes, stirring occasionally. Season to taste and sprinkle with parsley and cayenne pepper. Transfer to warm serving plates, garnish and serve immediately.

COOK'S TIP

For authenticity and flavour, use a few saffron strands soaked in a little boiling water instead of the turmeric. Saffron has a lovely, nutty flavour.

Lentil & Rice Casserole

This is a really hearty dish, perfect for cold days when a filling hot dish is just what you need.

Serves 4

INGREDIENTS

- 225 g/8 oz/$1^{1}/_{4}$ cups red split lentils
- 50 g/$1^{3}/_{4}$ oz/$^{1}/_{3}$ cup long-grain white rice
- 1 litre/$1^{3}/_{4}$ pints/5 cups vegetable stock
- 150 ml/$^{1}/_{4}$ pint/$^{2}/_{3}$ cup dry white wine
- 1 leek, cut into chunks
- 3 garlic cloves, crushed
- 400 g/14 oz can chopped tomatoes
- 1 tsp ground cumin
- 1 tsp chilli powder
- 1 tsp garam masala
- 1 red (bell) pepper, sliced
- 100 g/$3^{1}/_{2}$ oz small broccoli florets
- 8 baby corn cobs, halved lengthwise
- 50 g/$1^{3}/_{4}$ oz French (green) beans, halved
- 1 tbsp fresh basil, shredded
- salt and pepper
- fresh basil sprigs, to garnish

1 Place the lentils, rice, vegetable stock and white wine in a flameproof casserole dish and cook over a gentle heat for 20 minutes, stirring occasionally.

2 Add the leek, garlic, tomatoes, cumin, chilli powder, garam masala, (bell) pepper, broccoli, corn cobs and French (green) beans.

3 Bring the mixture to the boil, reduce the heat, cover and simmer for a further 10–15 minutes or until the vegetables are tender.

4 Add the shredded basil and season with salt and pepper to taste.

5 Garnish with fresh basil sprigs and serve immediately.

VARIATION

You can vary the rice in this recipe – use brown or wild rice, if you prefer.

Vegetable Hot Pot

In this recipe, a variety of vegetables are cooked under a layer of potatoes, topped with cheese and cooked until golden brown for a filling and tasty meal.

Serves 4

INGREDIENTS

- 2 large potatoes, thinly sliced
- 2 tbsp vegetable oil
- 1 red onion, halved and sliced
- 1 leek, sliced
- 2 garlic cloves, crushed
- 1 carrot, cut into chunks
- 100 g/3 1/2 oz broccoli florets
- 100 g/3 1/2 oz cauliflower florets
- 2 small turnips, quartered
- 1 tbsp plain (all-purpose) flour
- 700 ml/1 1/4 pints/3 1/2 cups vegetable stock
- 150 ml/1/4 pint/2/3 cup dry cider
- 1 dessert (eating) apple, sliced
- 2 tbsp chopped sage
- pinch of cayenne pepper
- 50 g/1 3/4 oz/1/2 cup vegetarian Cheddar cheese, grated
- salt and pepper

1 Cook the potato slices in a saucepan of boiling water for 10 minutes. Drain thoroughly and reserve.

2 Heat the oil in a flameproof casserole dish and sauté the onion, leek and garlic for 2–3 minutes. Add the remaining vegetables and cook for a further 3–4 minutes, stirring.

3 Stir in the flour and cook for 1 minute. Gradually add the stock and cider and bring the mixture to the boil. Add the apple, sage and cayenne pepper and season well. Remove the dish from the heat. Transfer the vegetables to an ovenproof dish.

4 Arrange the potato slices on top of the vegetable mixture to cover.

5 Sprinkle the cheese on top of the potato slices and cook in a preheated oven, 190°C/375°F/Gas Mark 5, for 30–35 minutes or until the potato is golden brown and beginning to crispen slightly around the edges. Serve immediately.

COOK'S TIP

If the potato begins to brown too quickly, cover with foil for the last 10 minutes of cooking time to prevent the top from burning.

Vegetable Toad-in-the-hole

This dish can be made in one large dish or in individual Yorkshire pudding tins (pans).

Serves 4

INGREDIENTS

BATTER:
100 g/3 1/2 oz/3/4 cup plain (all-purpose) flour
2 eggs, beaten
200 ml/7 fl oz/3/4 cup milk
2 tbsp wholegrain mustard
2 tbsp vegetable oil

FILLING:
2 tbsp butter
2 garlic cloves, crushed
1 onion, cut into eight
75 g/2 3/4 oz baby carrots, halved lengthwise
50 g/1 3/4 oz French (green) beans
50 g/1 3/4 oz canned sweetcorn, drained
2 tomatoes, seeded and cut into chunks
1 tsp wholegrain mustard
1 tbsp chopped mixed herbs
salt and pepper

1 To make the batter, sieve the flour and a pinch of salt into a large bowl. Make a well in the centre and beat in the eggs and milk to make a batter. Stir in the mustard and leave to stand.

2 Pour the oil into a shallow ovenproof dish and heat in a preheated oven, 200°C/400°F/ Gas Mark 6, for 10 minutes.

3 To make the filling, melt the butter in a frying pan (skillet) and sauté the garlic and onion for 2 minutes, stirring. Cook the carrots and beans in a saucepan of boiling water for 7 minutes or until tender. Drain well.

4 Add the sweetcorn and tomato to the frying pan (skillet) with the mustard and herbs. Season well and add the carrots and beans.

5 Remove the dish from the oven and pour in the batter. Spoon the vegetables into the centre, return to the oven and cook for 30–35 minutes until the batter has risen and set. Serve the vegetable toad-in-the-hole immediately.

COOK'S TIP

It is important that the oil is hot before adding the batter so that the batter begins to cook and rise immediately.

1

5

5

Vegetable Biryani

The Biryani originated in the North of India, and was a dish reserved for festivals. The vegetables are marinated in a yogurt-based marinade and cooked in a casserole dish with the rice and onions.

Serves 4

INGREDIENTS

1 large potato, cubed
100 g/3½ oz baby carrots
50 g/1¾ oz okra, thickly sliced
2 celery sticks, sliced
75 g/2¾ oz baby button mushrooms, halved
1 aubergine (eggplant), halved and sliced
300 ml/½ pint/1¼ cups natural (unsweetened) yogurt
1 tbsp grated root ginger
2 large onions, grated
4 garlic cloves, crushed
1 tsp turmeric
1 tbsp curry powder
2 tbsp butter
2 onions, sliced
225 g/8 oz/1¼ cups basmati rice
chopped coriander (cilantro), to garnish

1 Cook the potato cubes, carrots and okra in a pan of boiling salted water for 7–8 minutes. Drain well and place in a large bowl. Mix with the celery, mushrooms and aubergine (eggplant).

2 Mix the natural (unsweetened) yogurt, ginger, grated onions, garlic, turmeric and curry powder and spoon over the vegetables. Leave to marinate for at least 2 hours.

3 Heat the butter in a frying pan (skillet) and cook the sliced onions for 5–6 minutes until golden brown. Remove a few onions from the pan and reserve for garnishing.

4 Cook the rice in a pan of boiling water for 7 minutes. Drain well.

5 Add the marinated vegetables to the onions and cook for 10 minutes.

6 Put half of the rice in a 2 litre/3½ pint casserole dish. Spoon the vegetables on top and cover with the remaining rice. Cover and cook in a preheated oven, 190°C/375°F/Gas Mark 5, for 20–25 minutes or until the rice is tender.

7 Spoon the biryani on to a serving plate, garnish with the reserved onions and chopped coriander (cilantro) and serve immediately.

2

3

6

Artichoke & Cheese Tart

Artichoke hearts are delicious to eat, being very delicate in flavour and appearance. They are ideal for cooking in a cheese-flavoured pastry case.

Serves 8

INGREDIENTS

175 g/6 oz/1 1/4 cups wholemeal (whole wheat) flour
2 garlic cloves, crushed
75 g/2 3/4 oz/6 tbsp butter or vegetarian margarine
salt and pepper

FILLING:
2 tbsp olive oil
1 red onion, halved and sliced
10 canned or fresh artichoke hearts
100 g/3 1/2 oz/1 cup vegetarian Cheddar, grated
50 g/1 3/4 oz/1/2 cup Gorgonzola cheese, crumbled
2 eggs, beaten
1 tbsp chopped fresh rosemary
150 ml/1/4 pint/2/3 cup milk

1 To make the pastry, sieve the flour into a mixing bowl, add a pinch of salt and the garlic. Rub in the butter until the mixture resembles breadcrumbs. Stir in 3 tablespoons of water and bring the mixture together to form a dough.

2 Roll the pastry out on a lightly floured surface to fit a 20cm/8 inch flan tin (pan). Prick the pastry with a fork.

3 Heat the oil in a frying pan (skillet) and sauté the onion for 3 minutes. Add the artichoke hearts and cook for a further 2 minutes.

4 Mix the cheeses with the beaten eggs, rosemary and milk. Stir in the drained artichoke mixture and season to taste.

5 Spoon the artichoke and cheese mixture into the pastry case and cook in a preheated oven, 200°C/400°F/Gas Mark 6, for 25 minutes or until cooked and set. Serve the flan hot or cold.

COOK'S TIP

Gently press the centre of the flan with your fingertip to test if it is cooked through. It should feel fairly firm, but not solid. If overcooked the flan will begin to 'weep'.

2

3

5

Cantonese Garden Vegetable Stir-Fry

This dish tastes as fresh as it looks. Try to get hold of baby vegetables as they look and taste so much better in this dish.

Serves 4

INGREDIENTS

2 tbsp peanut oil
1 tsp Chinese five-spice powder
75 g/2¾ oz baby carrots, halved
2 celery sticks, sliced
2 baby leeks, sliced
50 g/1¾ oz mangetout (snow peas)
4 baby courgettes (zucchini), halved lengthwise
8 baby corn cobs
225 g/8 oz firm marinated tofu (bean curd), cubed
4 tbsp fresh orange juice
1 tbsp clear honey
celery leaves and orange zest, to garnish
cooked rice or noodles, to serve

1 Heat the oil in a preheated wok until almost smoking. Add the Chinese five-spice powder, carrots, celery, leeks, mangetout (snow peas), courgettes (zucchini) and corn cobs and stir-fry for 3–4 minutes.

2 Add the tofu (bean curd) and cook for a further 2 minutes, stirring.

3 Stir in the orange juice and honey, reduce the heat and cook for 1–2 minutes.

4 Transfer the stir-fry to a serving dish, garnish with celery leaves and orange zest and serve with rice or noodles.

COOK'S TIP

Chinese five-spice powder is a mixture of fennel, star anise, cinnamon bark, cloves and Szechuan pepper. It is very pungent so should be used sparingly. If kept in an airtight container, it will keep indefinitely.

VARIATION

Lemon juice would be just as delicious as the orange juice in this recipe, but use 3 tablespoons instead of 4 tablespoons.

Cheese & Potato Layer Bake

This really is a great side dish, perfect for serving with main meals cooked in the oven.

Serves 4

INGREDIENTS

450 g/1 lb potatoes
1 leek, sliced
3 garlic cloves, crushed
50 g/1¾ oz/½ cup Cheddar, grated
50 g/1¾ oz/½ cup Mozzarella, grated
25 g/1 oz/¼ cup Parmesan cheese, grated
2 tbsp chopped parsley
150 ml/¼ pint/⅔ cup single (light) cream
150 ml/¼ pint/⅔ cup milk
salt and pepper
freshly chopped flat-leaf parsley, to garnish

1 Cook the potatoes in a saucepan of boiling salted water for 10 minutes. Drain well.

2 Cut the potatoes into thin slices. Arrange a layer of potatoes in the base of an ovenproof dish. Layer with a little of the leek, garlic, cheeses and parsley. Season well.

3 Repeat the layers until all of the ingredients have been used, finishing with a layer of cheese on top.

4 Mix the cream and milk together, season with salt and pepper to taste and pour over the potato layers.

5 Cook in a preheated oven, 160°C/325°F/Gas Mark 3, for 1–1¼ hours or until the cheese is golden brown and bubbling and the potatoes are cooked through.

6 Garnish with freshly chopped flat-leaf parsley and serve immediately.

COOK'S TIP

Stir the vegetables occasionally during the 30 minutes cooking time to prevent them sticking to the bottom of the pan. If the liquid has not evaporated by the end of the cooking time, remove the lid and boil rapidly until the dish is dry.

2

2

4

Aubergine (Eggplant) & Courgette (Zucchini) Galette

This is a dish of aubergine (eggplant) and courgettes (zucchini) layered with a quick tomato sauce and melted cheese.

Serves 4

INGREDIENTS

2 large aubergines (eggplants), sliced
4 courgettes (zucchini)
2 x 400 g/14 oz cans chopped tomatoes, drained
2 tbsp tomato purée (paste)
2 garlic cloves, crushed
50 ml/2 fl oz/4 tbsp olive oil
1 tsp caster (superfine) sugar
2 tbsp chopped basil
olive oil, for frying
225 g/8 oz Mozzarella cheese, sliced
salt and pepper
fresh basil leaves, to garnish

1 Put the aubergine (eggplant) slices in a colander and sprinkle with salt. Leave to stand for 30 minutes, then rinse well under cold water and drain. Thinly slice the courgettes (zucchini).

2 Meanwhile, put the tomatoes, tomato purée (paste), garlic, olive oil, sugar and chopped basil into a pan and simmer for 20 minutes or until reduced by half. Season well.

3 Heat 2 tablespoons of olive oil in a large frying pan (skillet) and cook the aubergine (eggplant) slices for 2–3 minutes until just beginning to brown. Remove from the pan.

4 Add a further 2 tablespoons of oil to the pan and fry the courgette (zucchini) slices until browned.

5 Lay half of the aubergine (eggplant) slices in the base of an ovenproof dish. Top with half of the tomato sauce and the courgettes (zucchini) and then half of the Mozzarella.

6 Repeat the layers and bake in a preheated oven, 180°C/350°F/Gas Mark 4, for 45–50 minutes or until the vegetables are tender. Garnish with basil leaves and serve.

2

Greek Green Beans

This dish contains many Greek flavours such as lemon, garlic, oregano and olives, for a really flavourful recipe.

Serves 4

INGREDIENTS

- 400 g/14 oz can haricot (navy) beans, drained
- 1 tbsp olive oil
- 3 garlic cloves, crushed
- 425 ml/$^3/_4$ pint/2 cups vegetable stock
- 1 bay leaf
- 2 sprigs oregano
- 1 tbsp tomato purée (paste)
- juice of 1 lemon
- 1 small red onion, chopped
- 25 g/1 oz pitted black olives, halved
- salt and pepper

1 Put the haricot (navy) beans in a flameproof casserole dish.

2 Add the olive oil and crushed garlic and cook over a gentle heat, stirring occasionally, for 4–5 minutes.

3 Add the stock, bay leaf, oregano, tomato purée (paste), lemon juice and red onion, cover and simmer for about 1 hour or until the sauce has thickened.

4 Stir in the olives, season with salt and pepper to taste and serve.

VARIATION

You can substitute other canned beans for the haricot (navy) beans – try cannellini or black-eyed beans (peas), or chick-peas (garbanzo beans) instead. Remember to drain and rinse them thoroughly before use as canned beans often have sugar or salt added.

COOK'S TIP

This dish may be made in advance and served cold with crusty bread, if preferred.

Mini Vegetable Puff Pastry Cases

These are ideal with a more formal meal as they take a little time to prepare and look really impressive.

Serves 4

INGREDIENTS

450 g/1 lb puff pastry
1 egg, beaten

FILLING:
225 g/8 oz sweet potato, cubed
100 g/3½ oz baby asparagus spears
2 tbsp butter or vegetarian margarine
1 leek, sliced
2 small open-cap mushrooms, sliced
1 tsp lime juice
1 tsp chopped thyme
pinch of dried mustard
salt and pepper

1 Cut the pastry into 4 equal pieces. Roll each piece out on a lightly floured surface to form a 12.5 cm/5 inch square. Place on a dampened baking tray (cookie sheet) and score a smaller 7.5 cm/2.5 inch square inside.

2 Brush with beaten egg and cook in a preheated oven, 200°C/400°F/Gas Mark 6, for 20 minutes or until risen and golden brown.

3 Remove the pastry squares from the oven, then carefully cut out the central square of pastry, lift out and reserve.

4 To make the filling, cook the sweet potato in a saucepan of boiling water for 15 minutes, then drain well. Blanch the asparagus in a saucepan of boiling water for 10 minutes or until tender. Drain and reserve.

5 Melt the butter or margarine in a saucepan and sauté the leek and mushrooms for 2–3 minutes. Add the lime juice, thyme and mustard, season well and stir in the sweet potatoes and asparagus. Spoon into the pastry cases, top with the reserved pastry squares and serve immediately.

COOK'S TIP

Use a colourful selection of any vegetables you have at hand for this recipe.

This is a Parragon Book
First published in 2003

Parragon
Queen Street House
4 Queen Street, Bath, BA1 1HE, UK

All recipes and photography compiled from material created by 'Haldane Mason', and 'The Foundry'.

Cover design by Shelley Doyle.

ISBN: 1-40540-836-7

Printed in China

NOTE

This book uses imperial and metric measurements. Follow the same units of measurement throughout; do not mix imperial and metric. All spoon measurements are level; teaspoons are assumed to be 5 ml and tablespoons are assumed to be 15 ml. Unless otherwise stated, milk is assumed to be whole milk, eggs and individual vegetables such as potatoes are medium, and pepper is freshly ground black pepper.

The times given for each recipe are an approximate guide only because the preparation times may differ according to the techniques used by different people and the cooking times may vary as a result of the type of oven used.

Recipes using raw or very lightly cooked eggs should be avoided by infants, the elderly, pregnant women, convalescents and anyone suffering from an illness.